3

Happy House

Contents

Unit	Theme	Title
01	Cook	**Fry the Mushrooms and Carrots**
02	Appearances	**She Has Long Hair**
03	Favorite Things	**May I Have a Doll?**
04	Cities	**I Want to Visit New York**
05	Buildings	**Because I Want to See the Pyrami**
Review I (Units 01-05)		
06	Clothes	**I'm Wearing a Sweater**
07	Time	**It Takes Ten Minutes**
08	Rooms & Activities	**Where Is Mom?**
09	Weekend	**What Do You Do on Weekends?**
10	Subjects	**My Favorite Subject is Art**
Review II (Units 06-10)		

Words	Main Conversation
cut, add, stir, fry, onion, mushroom, carrot, cucumber	**A** Let's make fried rice. **B** *Fry* the *mushrooms* and *carrots*.
tall, short, long, curly, blond, black, pretty, handsome	**A** What does she look like? **B** She's *pretty*. She has *long hair*.
doll, robot, balloon, lollipop, shoes, chocolate, blocks, cake	**A** May I have a *doll*? **B** Yes, you may. / No, you may not.
New York, Cairo, Beijing, London, Sydney, Paris, Rome, Toronto	**A** Where do you want to visit? **B** I want to visit *New York*.
Statue of Liberty, Pyramid, Great Wall of China, Tower Bridge, Sydney Opera House, Eiffel Tower, Coliseum, CN Tower	**A** Why do you want to visit *Cairo*? **B** Because I want to see the *Pyramid*.
skirt, dress, shirt, jacket, sweater, pants, tie, socks	**A** What are you wearing? **B** I'm wearing a *sweater*.
minutes, hours, days, weeks, months, years, a long time, a little while	**A** How long does it take? **B** It takes ten *minutes*.
bedroom, living room, bathroom, kitchen, sleeping, watching TV, brushing his teeth, setting the table	**A** Where is Mom? **B** She's in the *bedroom*. She's *sleeping*.
go to the movies, visit my grandparents, read books, ride my bike, play soccer, meet my friends, go on picnics, use the computer	**A** What do you do on weekends? **B** I *go to the movies*.
science, math, history, music, gym, art, interesting, fun	**A** What is your favorite subject? **B** My favorite subject is *art*. *Art* is *interesting*.

How to Use This Book

Brainstorming

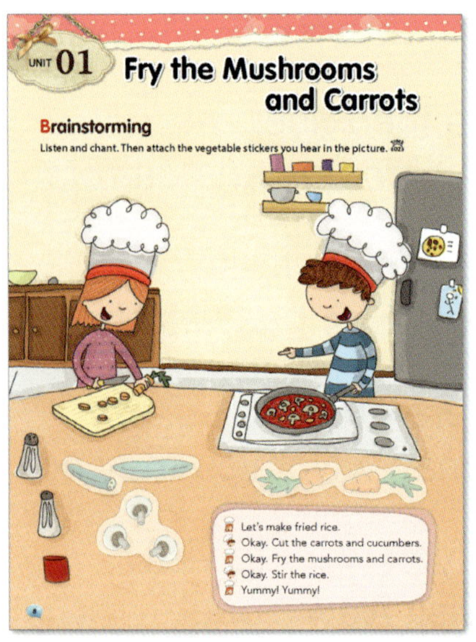

On this page is a short chant that introduces students to the vocabulary and sentence structures to be used throughout the unit. Here, students use stickers to isolate the vocabulary and practice chanting the key sentences.

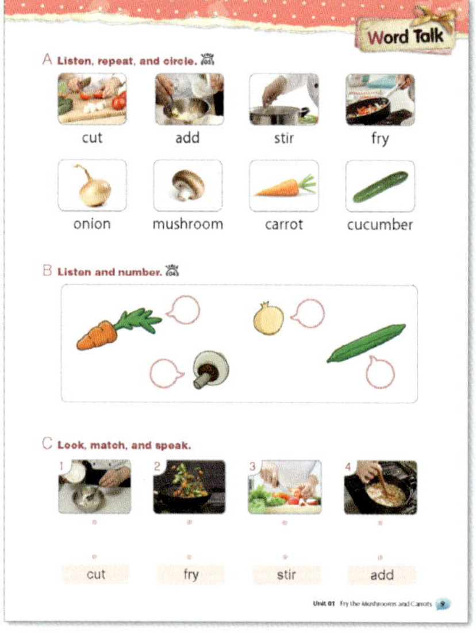

Word Talk

In this section, students practice the unit's vocabulary by repeating the words and then by doing listening and speaking exercises.

Sentence Talk

Students are again shown the sentence pattern in the form of a short dialog where they can substitute other vocabulary. Then, they use the sentences in two exercises, which encourage them to speak.

Role-Play

In this section, students really get talking by role-playing a situation with a friend. After role-playing practice, they do a short exercise which again asks them to role-play using the key sentence pattern.

Cartoon Dialog

Students listen to and repeat the cartoon dialog which contains everything they have learned in the unit. Afterward, they complete some comprehension questions which confirm their understanding of the unit material.

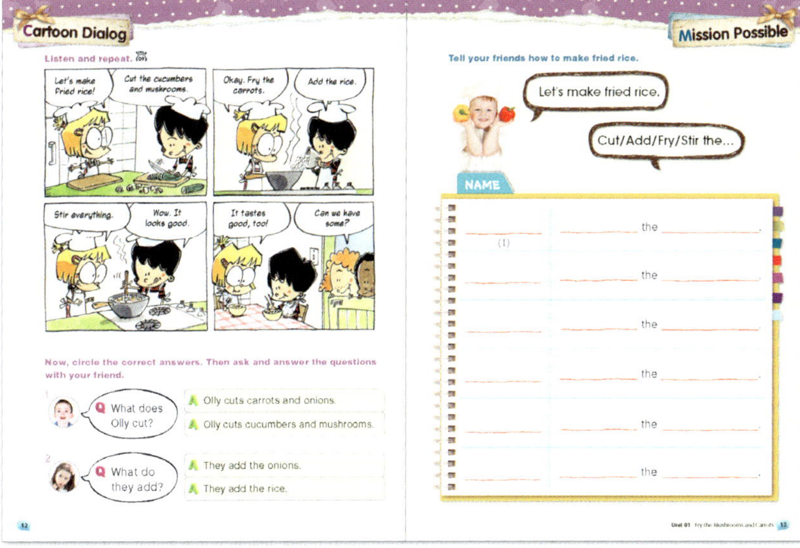

Mission Possible

In this last section, students ask each other questions independently and then share what they have learned with the class. By this point, students can confidently speak with their classmates and teachers in English.

Review

The review covers five units and gives students a chance to recall and practice the vocabulary and sentence patterns.

Workbook

These are useful exercises that students can either do independently or as a class to practice what they have learned.

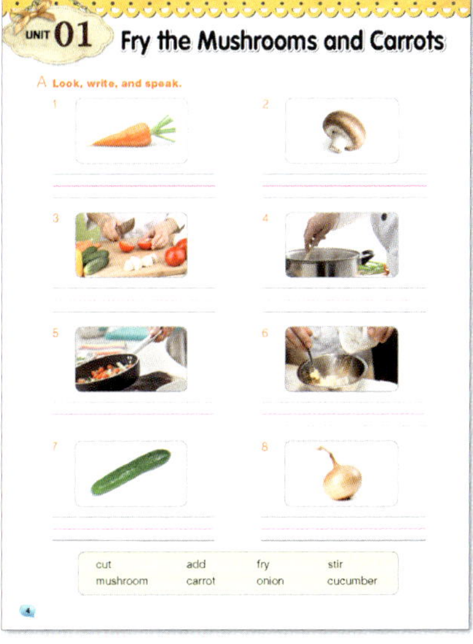

Fry the Mushrooms and Carrots

Brainstorming

Listen and chant. Then attach the vegetable stickers you hear in the picture. Track 02

A Listen, repeat, and circle. Track 03

cut

add

stir

fry

onion

mushroom

carrot

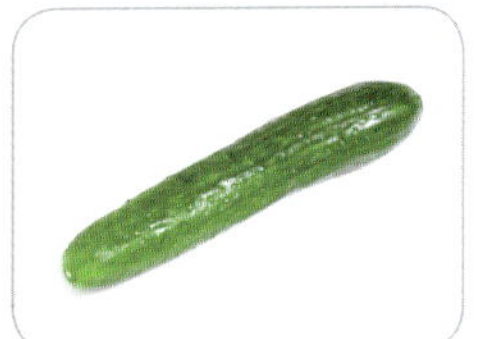
cucumber

B Listen and number. Track 04

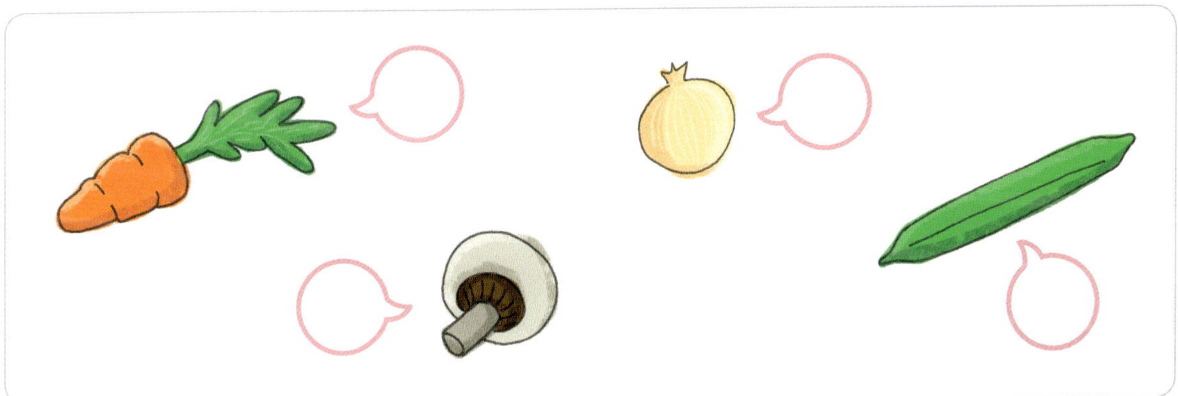

C Look, match, and speak.

1

2

3

4

cut   fry   stir   add

A Listen and repeat. Track 05

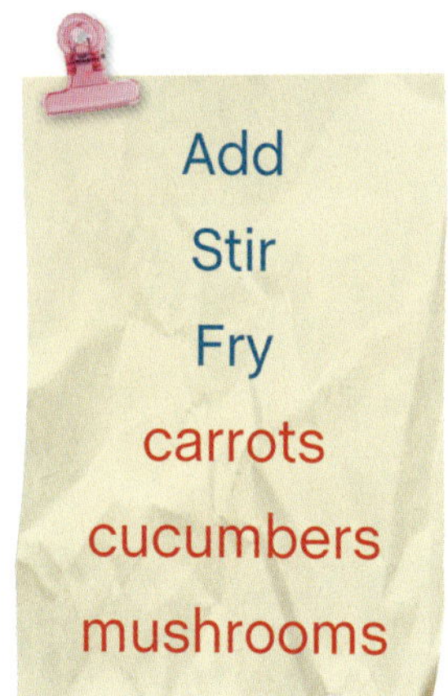

B Listen, match, and speak. Track 06

1 

Cut •

• the mushrooms.

2 

Add •

• the cucumbers.

3 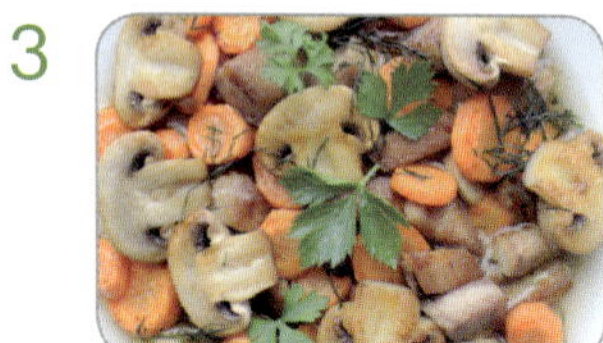

Fry •

• the mushrooms and carrots.

C Listen, check(✓), and speak. Track 07

A Listen and repeat. Then role-play with your friend. Track 08

B Look and write. Then role-play with your friend.

1

A ______________ make fried rice.

B Cut the ______________.

2

A Let's ______________ fried rice.

B ______________ the mushrooms and onions.

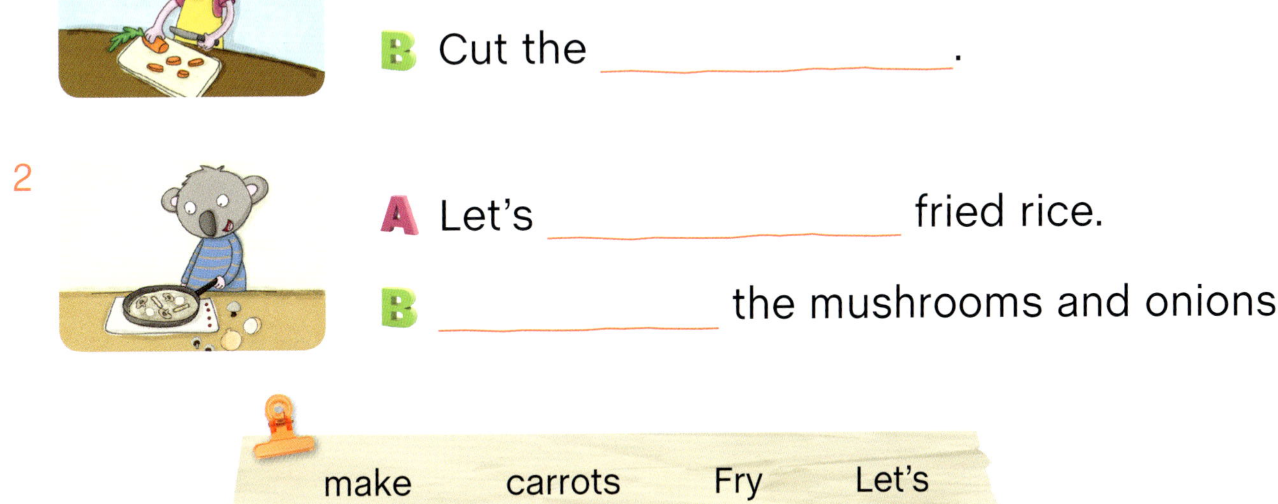

Listen and repeat. Track 09

Now, circle the correct answers. Then ask and answer the questions with your friend.

1 

Q What does Olly cut?

A Olly cuts carrots and onions.

A Olly cuts cucumbers and mushrooms.

2 

Q What do they add?

A They add the onions.

A They add the rice.

Tell your friends how to make fried rice.

Let's make fried rice.

Cut/Add/Fry/Stir the...

NAME

(I)

the ________ .

the ________ .

the ________ .

the ________ .

the ________ .

the ________ .

She Has Long Hair

Brainstorming

Listen and chant. Then attach the people stickers you hear in the picture. Track 10

A Listen, repeat, and circle. Track 11

tall

short

long

curly

blond

black

pretty

handsome

B Listen and number. Track 12

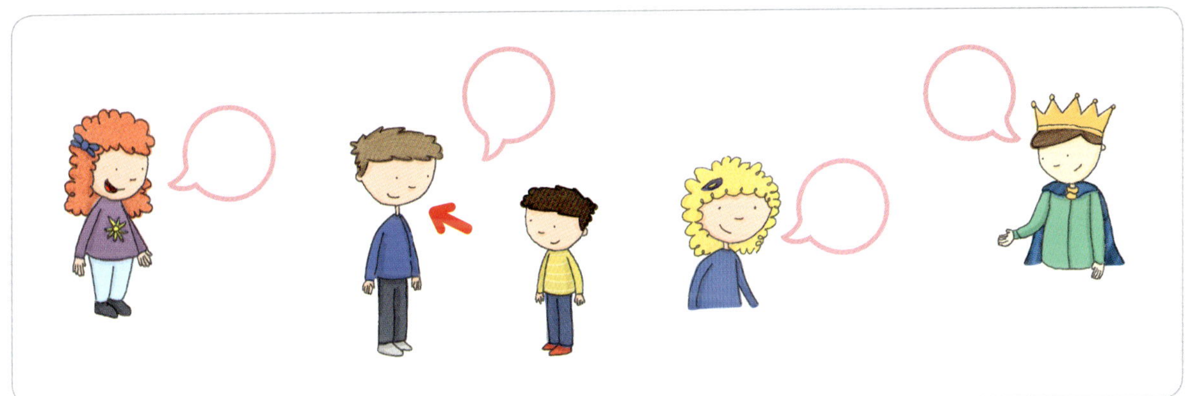

C Look, circle, and speak.

1
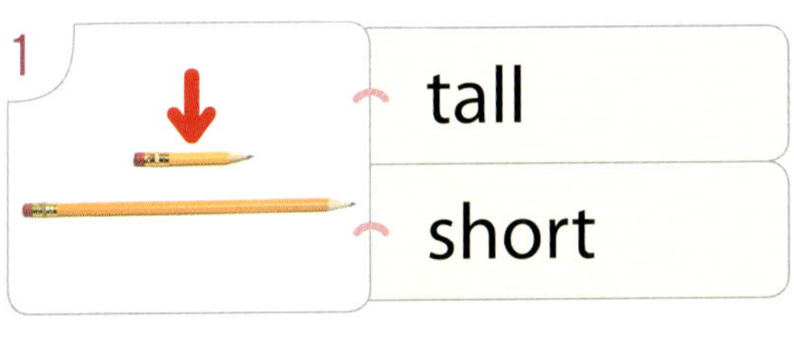
tall
short

2

long
curly

3

pretty
handsome

4

blond
black

A Listen and repeat. Track 13

B Listen, circle, and speak. Track 14

1 
She's (handsome | pretty).
She has (blond | brown) hair.

2 
He's (tall | short).
He has (brown | black) hair.

3 
She's (short | tall).
She has (blond | black) hair.

C Listen, draw, and speak. Track 15

1 

2 

3 

A Listen and repeat. Then role-play with your friend. Track 16

B Look and write. Then role-play with your friend.

1

Q What does she look like?

A She's __________. She has __________ hair.

2

Q What does he __________ like?

A He's tall. He has __________ hair.

curly   look   black   short

Listen and repeat. Track 17

Now, circle the correct answers. Then ask and answer the questions with your friend.

1 

Q What does the singer look like?

A He has blond hair.

A He has brown hair.

2

Q Is he tall or short?

A He is tall.

A He is short.

Think about your best friend. Then ask and answer the questions with your friends.

NAME

__________ (I)	__________ is __________ . He/She has __________ hair.
__________	__________ is __________ . He/She has __________ hair.
__________	__________ is __________ . He/She has __________ hair.
__________	__________ is __________ . He/She has __________ hair.

Now, tell the class about their best friends.

Teacher What does __________ 's best friend look like?

I __________ is __________ .

He/She has __________ hair.

May I Have a Doll?

Brainstorming

Listen and chant. Then attach the object stickers you hear in the picture. Track 18

A Listen, repeat, and circle. Track 19

doll

robot

balloon

lollipop

shoes

chocolate

blocks

cake

B Listen and number. Track 20

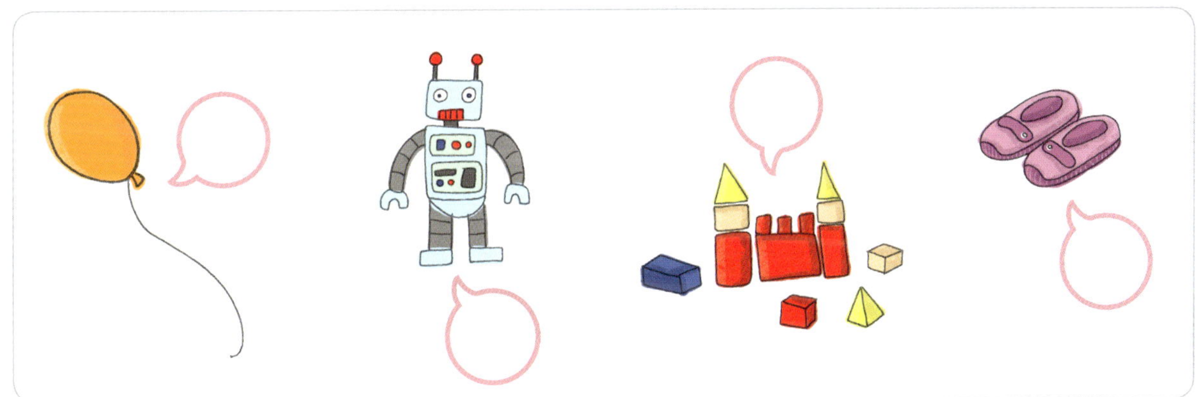

C Look, circle, and speak.

1
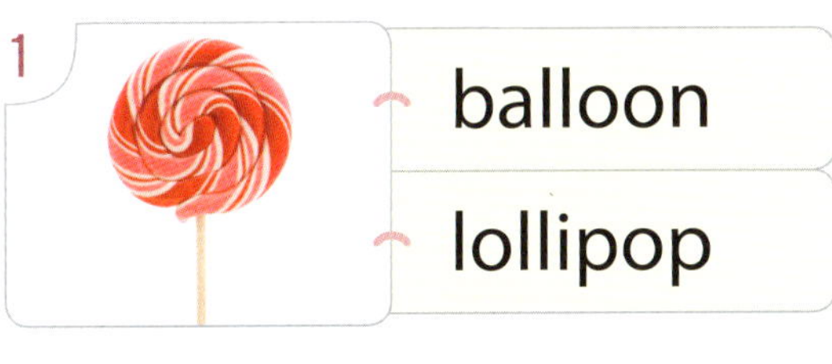
balloon
lollipop

2

doll
blocks

3
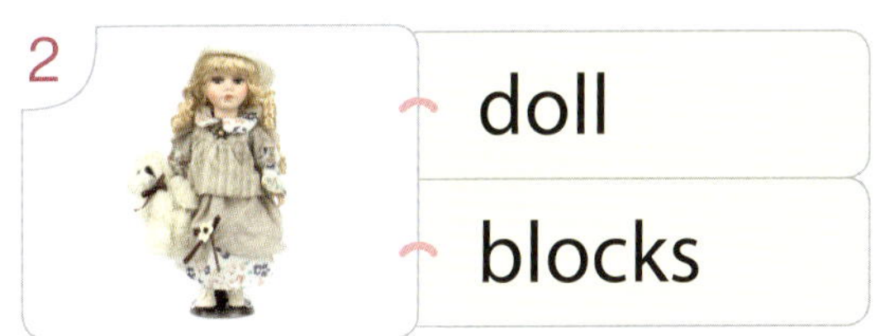
cake
shoes

4
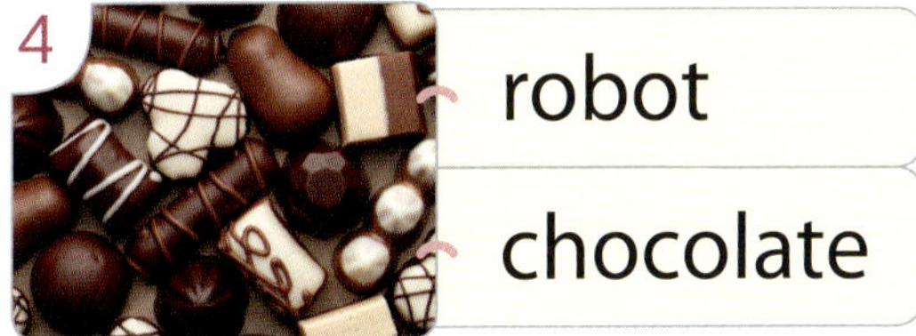
robot
chocolate

A **Listen and repeat.** Track 21

B **Listen, match, and speak.** Track 22

1 May I have •

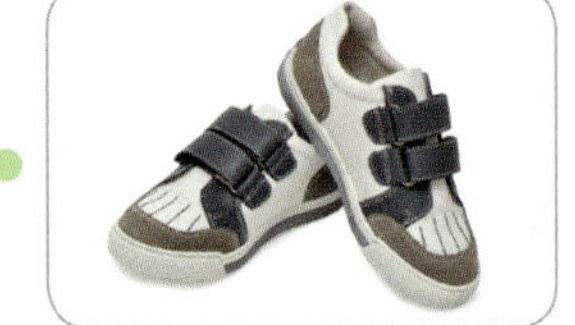

• a doll?

2 May I have •

• some shoes?

3 May I have •

• some chocolate?

C **Listen and circle O or X.** Track 23

1

O   X

2

O   X

3

O   X

A Listen and repeat. Then role-play with your friend. (Track 24)

B Look and write. Then role-play with your friend.

1

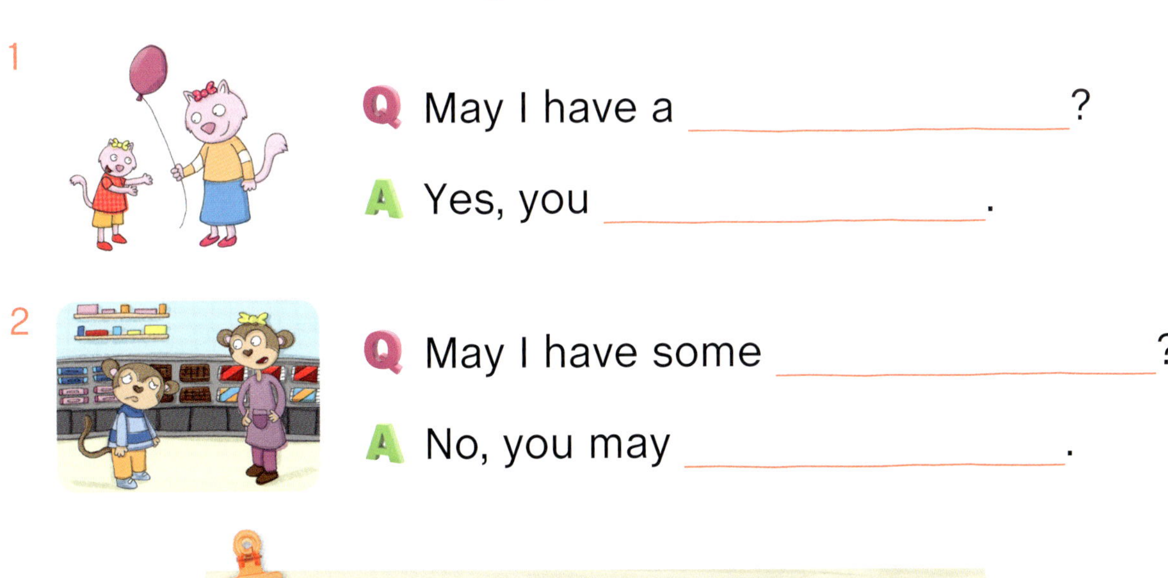

Q May I have a _______________?

A Yes, you _______________.

2

Q May I have some _______________?

A No, you may _______________.

chocolate   not   balloon   may

Listen and repeat. Track 25

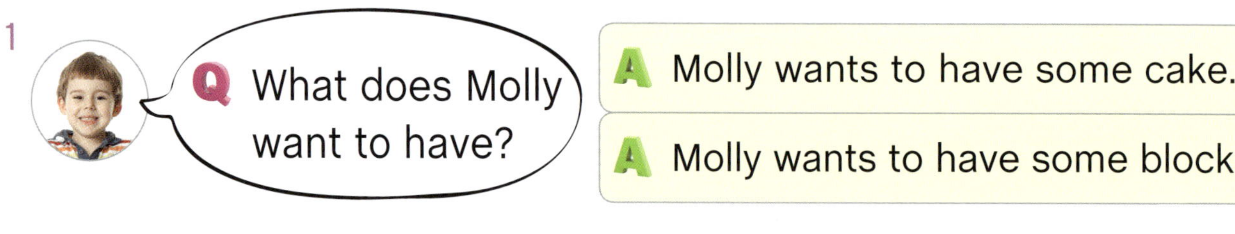

Now, circle the correct answers. Then ask and answer the questions with your friend.

1

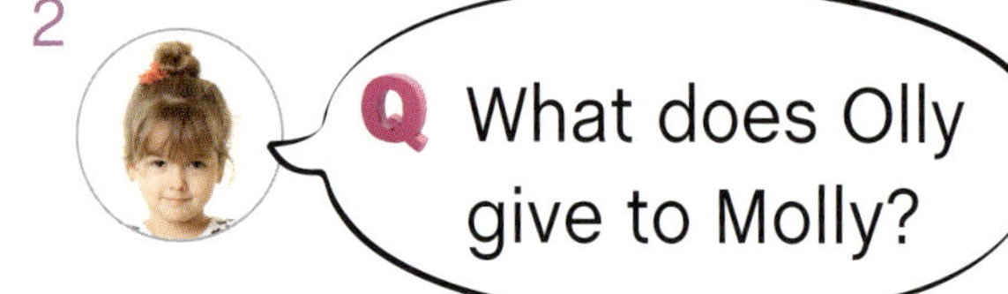

Q What does Molly want to have?

A Molly wants to have some cake.

A Molly wants to have some blocks.

2

Q What does Olly give to Molly?

A Olly gives her a robot.

A Olly gives her a balloon.

Ask and answer the questions with your friends.

ASK	ANSWER
May I have _______?	_______.
May I have _______?	_______.
May I have _______?	_______.
May I have _______?	_______.
May I have _______?	_______.
May I have _______?	_______.

I Want to Visit New York

Brainstorming

Listen and chant. Then attach the city stickers you hear in the picture. Track 26

A Listen, repeat, and circle. Track 27

New York

Cairo

Beijing

London

Sydney

Paris

Rome

Toronto

B Listen and number. Track 28

C Look, circle, and speak.

1 
Sydney
New York

2 
Paris
Toronto

3 
Rome
London

4 
Beijing
Cairo

A Listen and repeat. Track 29

B Listen, circle, and speak. Track 30

1 

I want to visit (London | Toronto).

2 

I want to visit (Sydney | Rome).

3 

I want to visit (New York | Beijing).

C Listen and circle O or X. Track 31

1 

O X

2 

O X

3 

O X

A Listen and repeat. Then role-play with your friend. Track 32

B Look and write. Then role-play with your friend.

1

Q _______________ do you want to visit?

A I want to visit _______________.

2

Q Where do you want to _______________?

A I want to visit _______________.

London   visit   New York   Where

Listen and repeat. (Track 33)

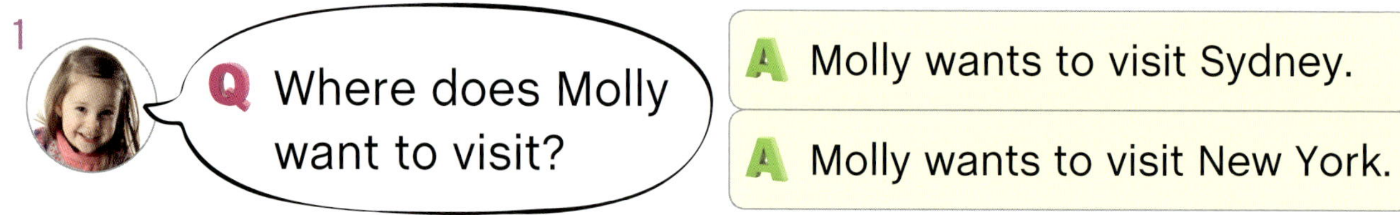

Now, circle the correct answers. Then ask and answer the questions with your friend.

1
Q Where does Molly want to visit?

A Molly wants to visit Sydney.

A Molly wants to visit New York.

2 
Q Where does Olly want to visit?

A Olly wants to visit Rome.

A Olly wants to visit Toronto.

Ask and answer the questions with your friends.

	I want to visit __________.
(I)	
	I want to visit __________.
	I want to visit __________.
	I want to visit __________.

Now, tell the class about your friends.

Teacher   Where does your friend want to visit?

I __________ wants to visit __________.

Because I Want to See the Pyramid

Brainstorming

Listen and chant. Then attach the building stickers you hear in the picture. Track 34

A Listen, repeat, and circle. Track 35

Statue of Liberty

Pyramid

Great Wall of China

Tower Bridge

Sydney Opera House

Eiffel Tower

Coliseum

CN Tower

B Listen and number. Track 36

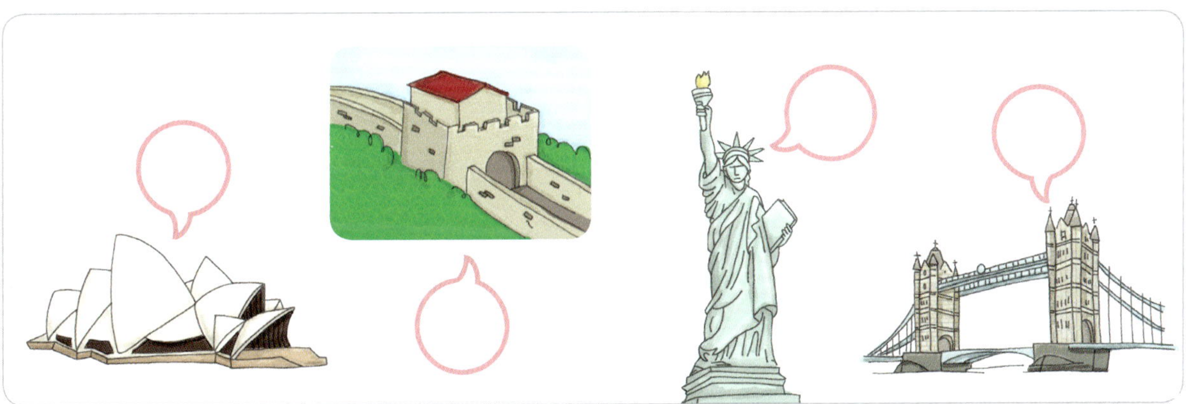

C Look, circle, and speak.

1 
Statue of Liberty
Eiffel Tower

2 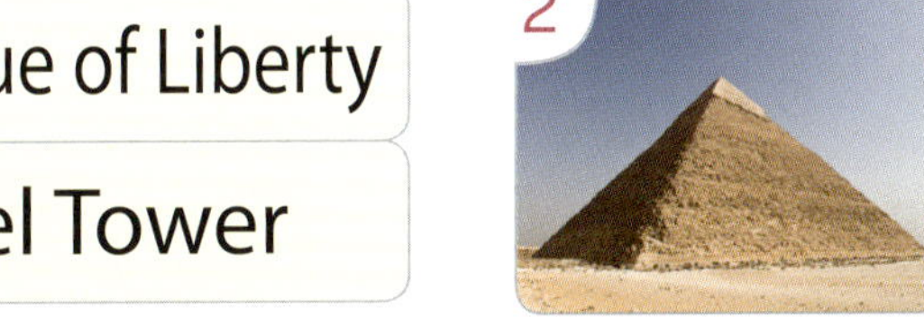
Great Wall of China
Pyramid

3 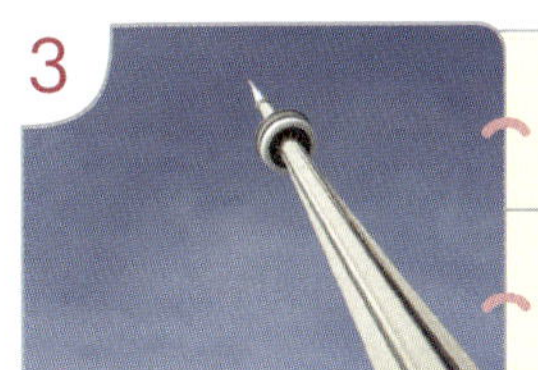
CN Tower
Tower Bridge

4 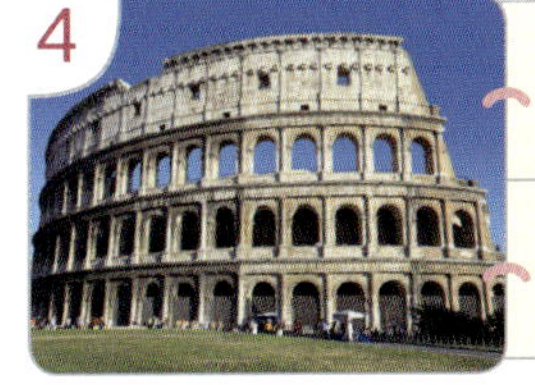
Coliseum
Sydney Opera House

A Listen and repeat. Track 37

B Listen, match, and speak. Track 38

1 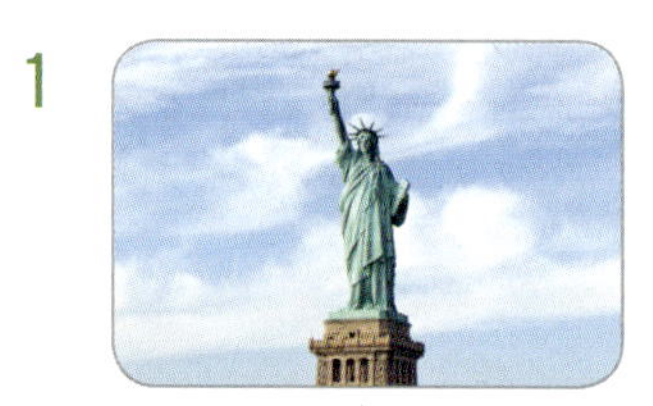

2

3

Because I want to see the Coliseum.

Because I want to see the Eiffel Tower.

Because I want to see the Statue of Liberty.

C Listen, check(✔), and speak. Track 39

A Listen and repeat. Then role-play with your friend. Track 40

B Look and write. Then role-play with your friend.

1

Q Why do you want to _____________ New York?

A Because I want to see the _____________.

2

Q _____________ do you want to visit Rome?

A _____________ I want to see the Coliseum.

Because   visit   Statue of Liberty   Why

Listen and repeat. (Track 41)

Now, circle the correct answers. Then ask and answer the questions with your friend.

1

Q Why does Molly want to visit Beijing?

A Because she wants to see the Great Wall of China.

A Because she wants to see the Eiffel Tower.

2

Q Why does Olly want to visit Rome?

A Because he wants to see the Pyramid.

A Because he wants to see the Coliseum.

Mission Possible

Ask and answer the questions with your friends.

NAME	CITY	
(I)		Because I want to see the ________.
		Because I want to see the ________.
		Because I want to see the ________.
		Because I want to see the ________.

Now, tell the class about your friends.

Teacher Why does your friend want to visit ________?

I Because ________ wants to see the ________.

Review I Units 01-05

A Find, circle, and match.

S	Y	D	N	E	Y	S	K
R	I	U	D	F	Y	H	R
H	O	E	R	A	D	O	P
C	U	C	U	M	B	E	R
I	B	A	K	L	P	S	J
N	D	A	T	A	L	L	R
L	C	U	E	A	K	K	E

B Listen, circle, and write. (Track 42)

1. 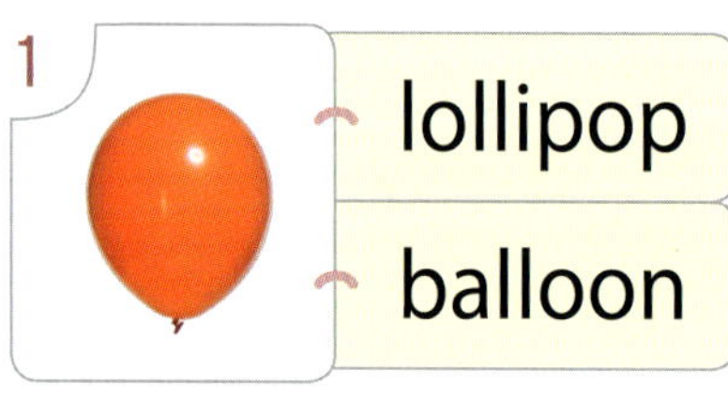
   - lollipop
   - balloon

2. 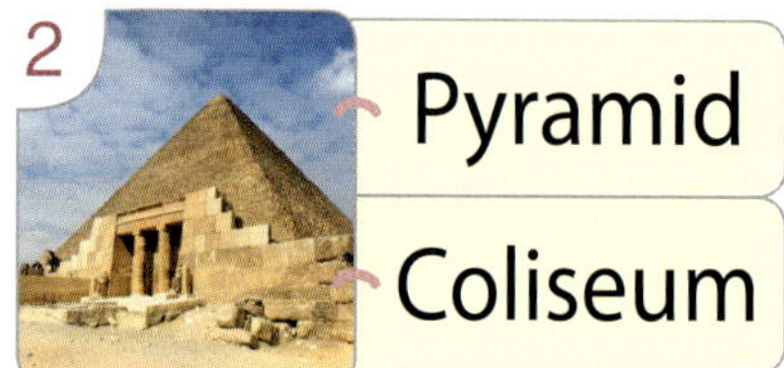
   - Pyramid
   - Coliseum

3. 
   - Paris
   - London

4. 
   - onion
   - mushroom

5. 
   - long
   - curly

6. 
   - cut
   - stir

C Look, read, and number.

❶ Cut the carrots.
❷ Fry the mushrooms and onions.
❸ May I have a balloon?
❹ Because I want to see the Coliseum.
❺ I want to visit New York.
❻ She's short. She has curly hair.

D Listen and write. Track 43

1    has   blond   She   hair

2    I   see   the Eiffel Tower   want to   Because

3    chocolate?   have   some   I   May

 Read, match, and speak.

1 

2

3

4

F **Listen and number.** (Track 44)

 Circle the words you find along the way and read the sentences. Then write the correct answer.

I'm Wearing a Sweater

Brainstorming

Listen and chant. Then attach the clothing stickers you hear in the picture. Track 45

What are you wearing?
I'm wearing a dress.
What are you wearing?
I'm wearing a shirt and pants.
What are you wearing?
I'm wearing a sweater.

A Listen, repeat, and circle. Track 46

skirt

dress

shirt

jacket

sweater

pants

tie

socks

B Listen and number. Track 47

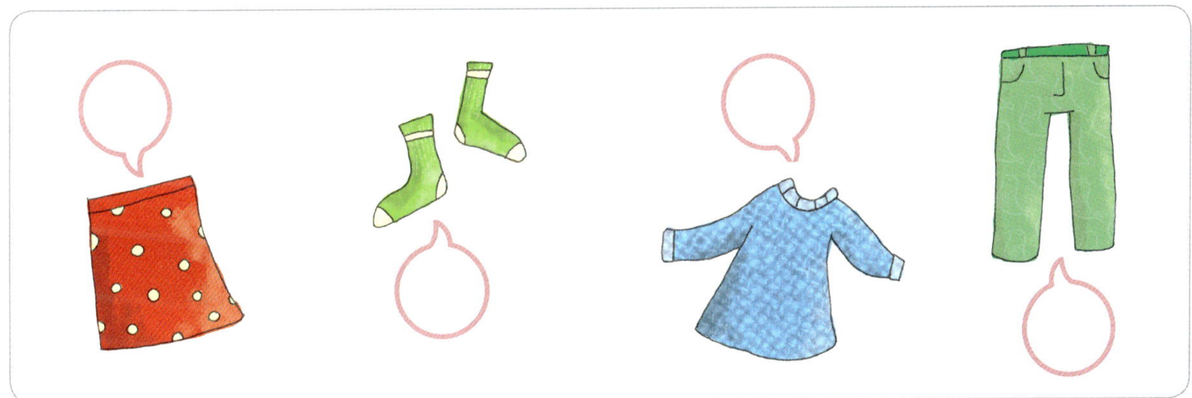

C Look, circle, and speak.

1

pants

dress

2

socks

tie

3

jacket

sweater

4

shirt

skirt

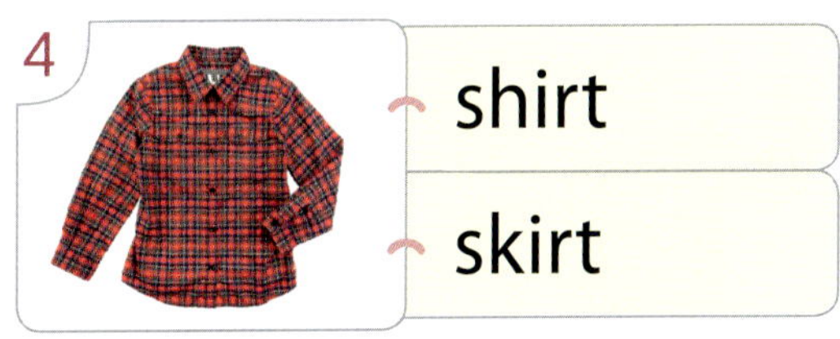

A Listen and repeat. Track 48

B Listen, circle, and speak. Track 49

1  I'm wearing a (pants **|** jacket).

2 I'm wearing a (dress **|** skirt).

3 I'm wearing a (sweater **|** tie) and pants.

C Listen, check(✓), and speak. Track 50

B Look and write. Then role-play with your friend.

1

Q What are you ______________?

A I'm wearing a ______________.

2

Q What are you wearing?

A I'm wearing a ______________ and

______________.

dress   jacket   wearing   pants

Listen and repeat. Track 52

Now, circle the correct answers. Then ask and answer the questions with your friend.

1

Q What is the girl wearing?

A She's wearing a shirt and pants.

A She's wearing a shirt and a jacket.

2

Q What is Molly wearing?

A Molly is wearing a skirt and socks.

A Molly is wearing a shirt and a skirt.

Ask and answer the questions with your friends.

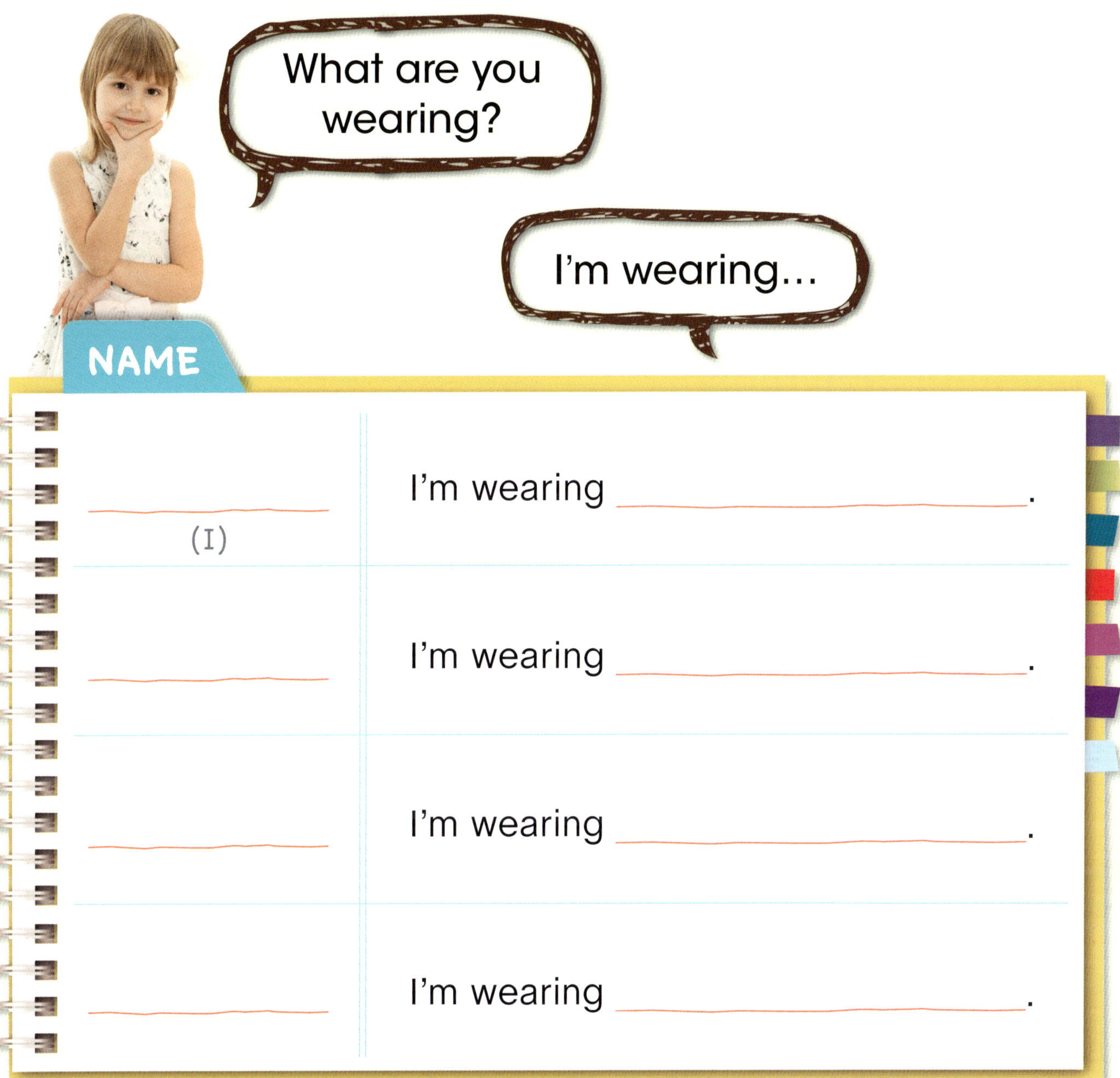

Now, tell the class about your friends.

Teacher   What is your friend wearing?

I   __________ is wearing __________ .

It Takes Ten Minutes

Brainstorming

Listen and chant. Then attach the picture stickers you hear in the picture. Track 53

A Listen, repeat, and circle. Track 54

minutes

hours

days

weeks

months

years

a long time

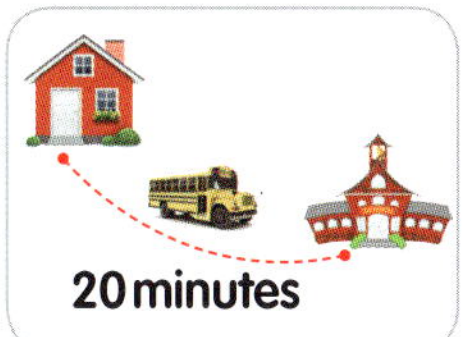

a little while

B Listen and number. Track 55

C Look, match, and speak.

a long time

months

a little while

years

A Listen and repeat. Track 56

B Listen, match, and speak. Track 57

1

2

3
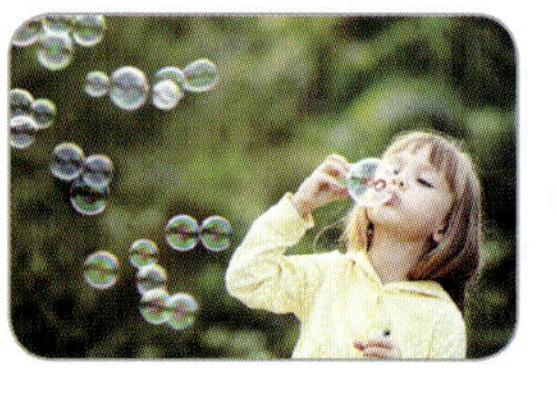

It takes one hour.

It takes ten months.

It takes five minutes.

C Listen, check(✓), and speak. Track 58

A Listen and repeat. Then role-play with your friend. Track 59

B Look and write. Then role-play with your friend.

1

Q How ____________ does it take?

A It takes ____________.

2

Q How long does it ____________?

A It takes ____________.

two hours   take   one week   long

Listen and repeat. (Track 60)

Now, circle the correct answers. Then ask and answer the questions with your friend.

1

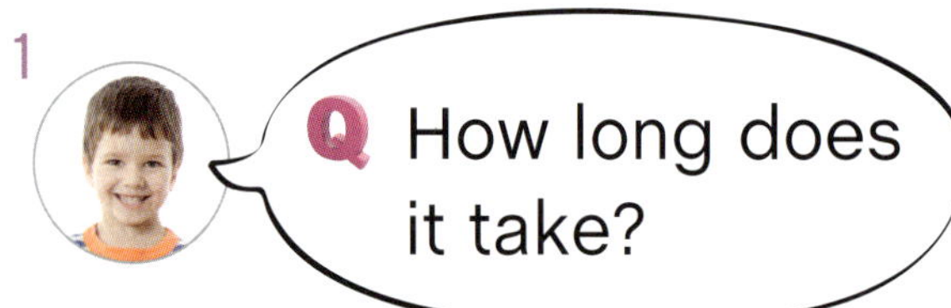

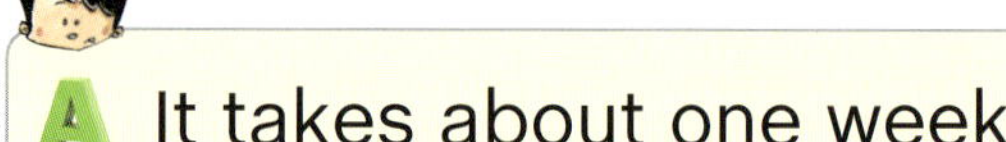

2

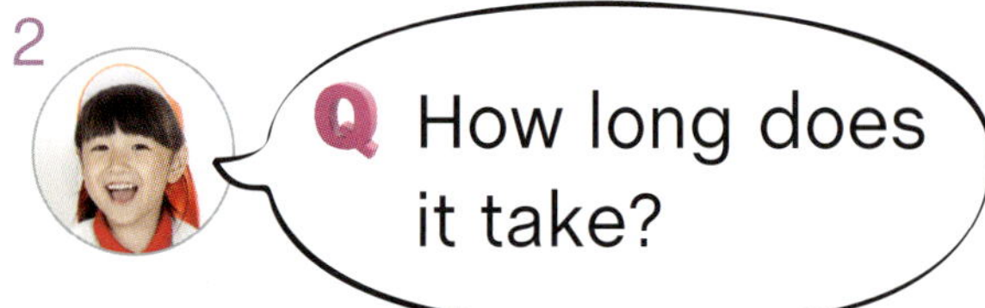

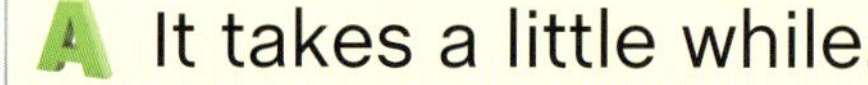

52

Think about reading a book. Then ask and answer the questions with your friends.

(I)	It takes __________ .
	It takes __________ .
	It takes __________ .
	It takes __________ .

Now, tell the class about your friends.

Teacher How long does it take?

I It takes __________ .

Where Is Mom?

Brainstorming

Listen and chant. Then attach the acting stickers you hear in the picture. Track 61

A Listen, repeat, and circle. Track 62

bedroom

living room

bathroom

kitchen

sleeping

watching TV

brushing his teeth

setting the table

B Listen and number. Track 63

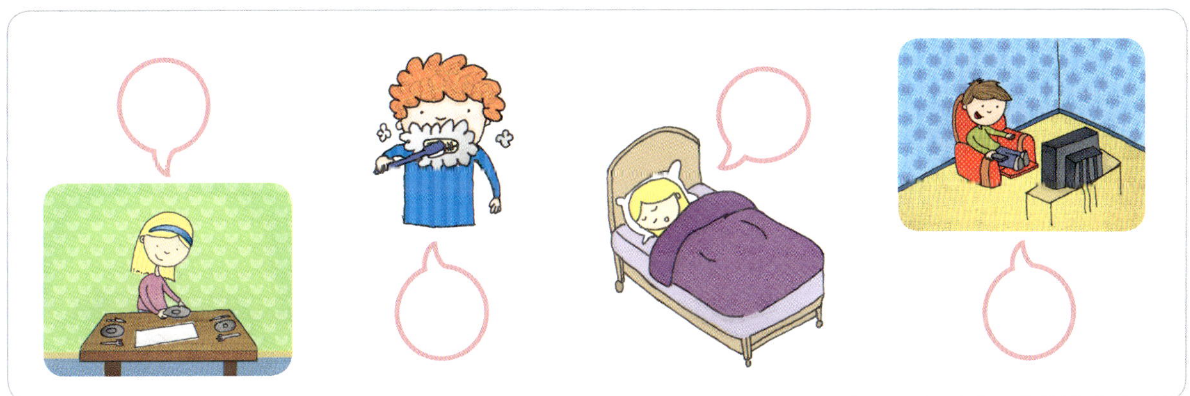

C Look, circle, and speak.

1 
living room
bathroom

2 
kitchen
bedroom

3 
kitchen
bedroom

4 
bathroom
living room

A Listen and repeat. Track 64

B Listen, match, and speak. Track 65

1. She's in the kitchen. •   • He's watching TV.

2. He's in the living room. •   • She's brushing her teeth.

3. She's in the bathroom. •   • She's setting the table.

C Listen and circle O or X. Track 66

1. 

O   X

2. 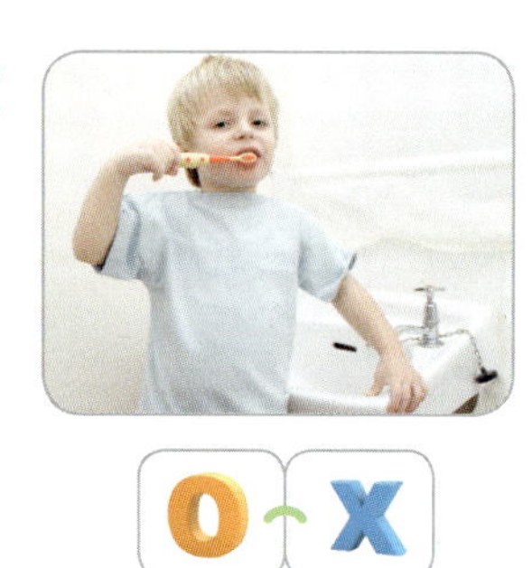

O   X

3. 

O   X

A Listen and repeat. Then role-play with your friend. Track 67

B Look and write. Then role-play with your friend.

1 

Q Where is your brother?

A He's in the ________________.
He's ________________.

2 

Q Where is your sister?

A She's in the ________________.
She's ________________ TV.

watching   bedroom   living room   sleeping

Cartoon Dialog

Listen and repeat. (Track 68)

Now, circle the correct answers. Then ask and answer the questions with your friend.

1 

2 

Imagine you are home in the evening. Ask and answer the questions with your friends.

NAME	
_______ (I)	I'm in the _______. I'm _______.
_______	I'm in the _______. I'm _______.
_______	I'm in the _______. I'm _______.
_______	I'm in the _______. I'm _______.

Now, tell the class about your friends.

Teacher	Where is your friend?
I	_______ is in the _______. He's/She's _______.

What Do You Do on Weekends?

Brainstorming

Listen and chant. Then attach the activity stickers you hear in the picture. Track 69

A Listen, repeat, and circle. (Track 70)

go to the movies

visit my grandparents

read books

ride my bike

play soccer

meet my friends

go on picnics

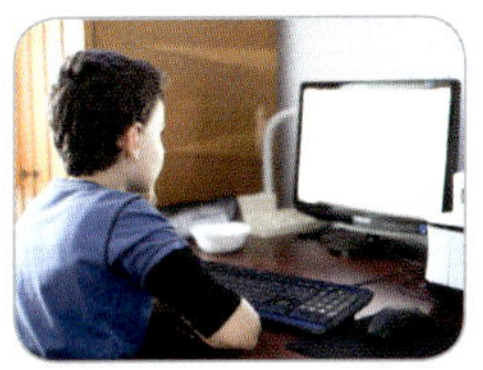
use the computer

B Listen and number. (Track 71)

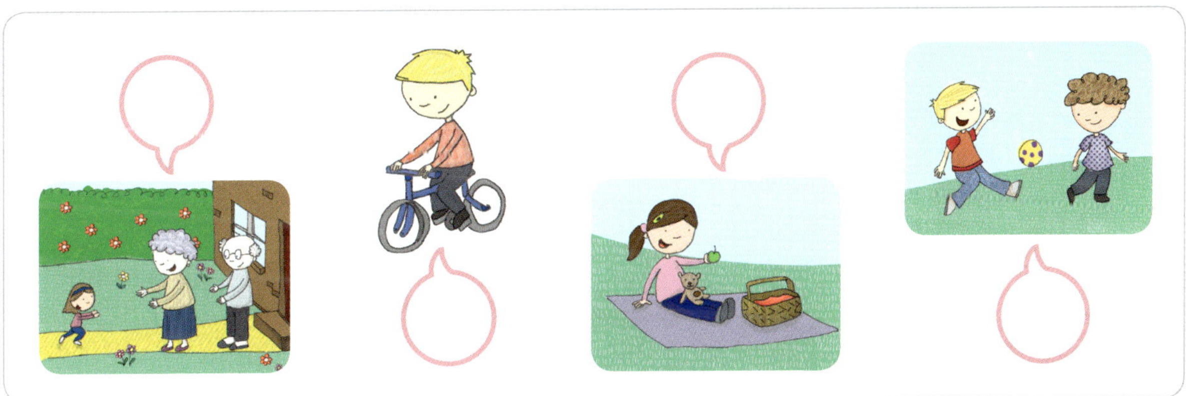

C Look, circle, and speak.

1 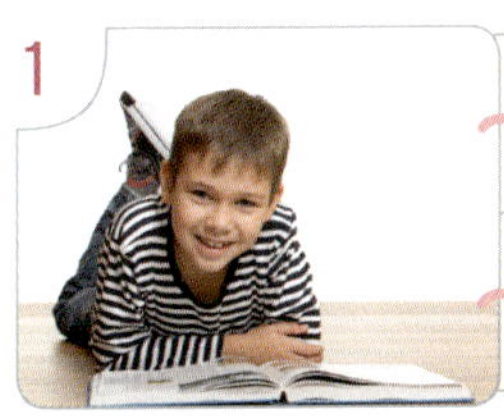
ride my bike
read books

2 
meet my friends
visit my grandparents

4 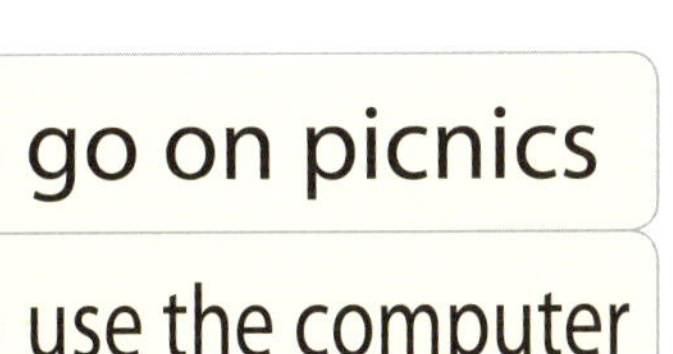
go on picnics
use the computer

3 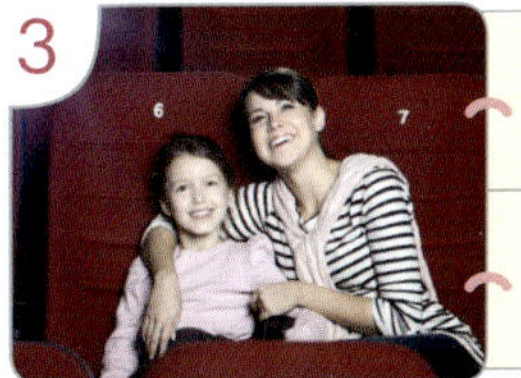
play soccer
go to the movies

A Listen and repeat. Track 72

B Listen, circle, and speak. Track 73

1 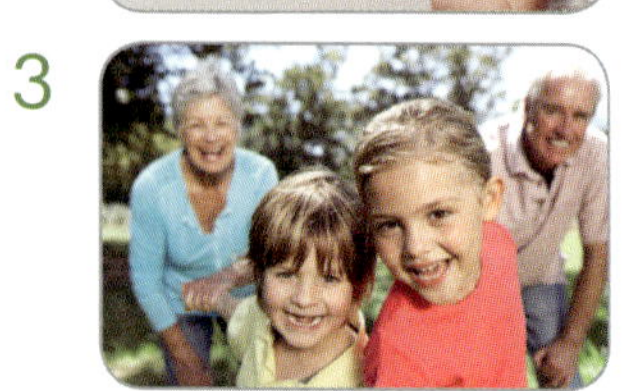 I (ride | read) my bike.

2 I (meet | use) the computer.

3  I (play | visit) my grandparents.

C Listen and circle O or X. Track 74

1  O X

2 O X

3  O X

A Listen and repeat. Then role-play with your friend. Track 75

B Look and write. Then role-play with your friend.

1
Q What do you do __________ weekends?

A I ____________________________.

2
Q What do you do on ____________________?

A I ____________________________.

play soccer   on   go on picnics   weekends

Listen and repeat. Track 76

Now, circle the correct answers. Then ask and answer the questions with your friend.

1  **Q** What does the boy do on weekends?

A He goes to the movies.

A He visits his grandparents.

2 **Q** What does Olly do on weekends?

A He rides his bike.

A He reads books.

Ask and answer the questions with your friends.

NAME

(I)

I ___________________________ .

I ___________________________ .

I ___________________________ .

I ___________________________ .

Now, tell the class about your friends.

Teacher　　What does your friend do on weekends?

I ___________________________

My Favorite Subject Is Art

Brainstorming

Listen and chant. Then attach the subject stickers you hear in the picture. Track 77

A Listen, repeat, and circle. Track 78

science

math

history

music

gym

art

interesting

fun

B Listen and number. Track 79

C Look, circle, and speak.

1 
music
history

2 
art
gym

3 
bored
interesting

4 
fun
sad

A Listen and repeat. Track 80

B Listen, match, and speak. Track 81

1.

My favorite subject is music. It's fun.

2.

My favorite subject is math. It's interesting.

3.

My favorite subject is gym. It's interesting.

C Listen, check(✓), and speak. Track 82

A **Listen and repeat. Then role-play with your friend.** Track 83

B **Look and write. Then role-play with your friend.**

1 

Q What is your favorite _____________?

A My favorite subject is _____________.
It's fun.

2 

Q What is your favorite subject?

A My favorite subject is _____________.
It's _____________.

science   interesting   music   subject

Cartoon Dialog

Now, circle the correct answers. Then ask and answer the questions with your friend.

1 **Q** What is Olly's favorite subject?

A His favorite subject is art.

A His favorite subject is music.

2 **Q** What is Molly's favorite subject?

A Her favorite subject is history.

A Her favorite subject is science.

Ask and answer the questions with your friends.

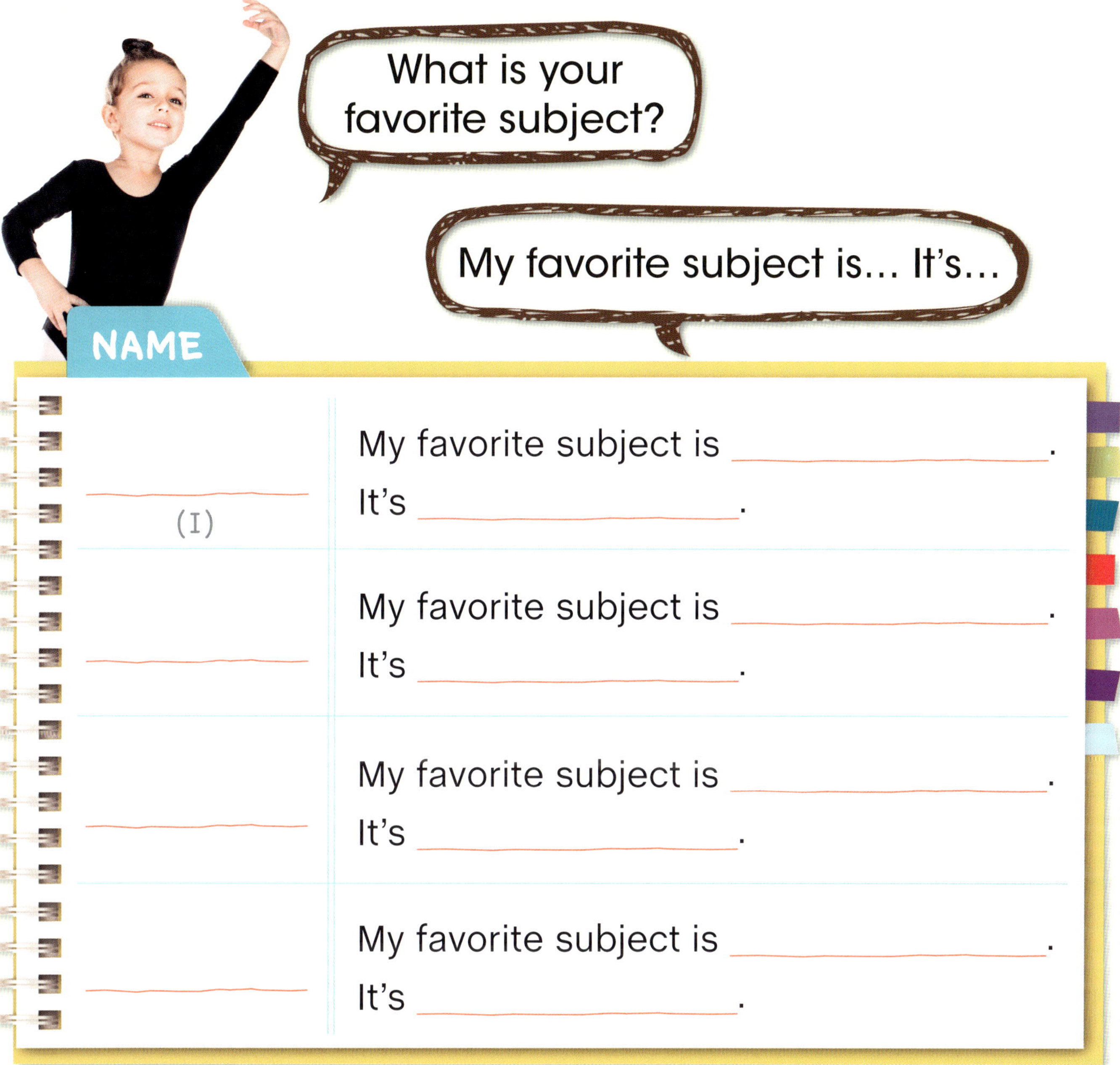

Now, tell the class about your friends.

Teacher   What is your friend's favorite subject?

I   _______________'s favorite subject is _______________.

It's _______________.

A Find, circle, and match.

1 

2

3

4

P	F	E	B	M	S	I	Y
Z	P	A	M	T	C	X	D
S	L	E	E	P	I	N	G
O	K	O	G	A	E	T	S
C	S	O	C	N	N	I	K
I	T	A	K	T	C	P	C
S	O	C	K	S	E	O	E

B Listen, circle, and write. (Track 85)

1 
- math
- art

2 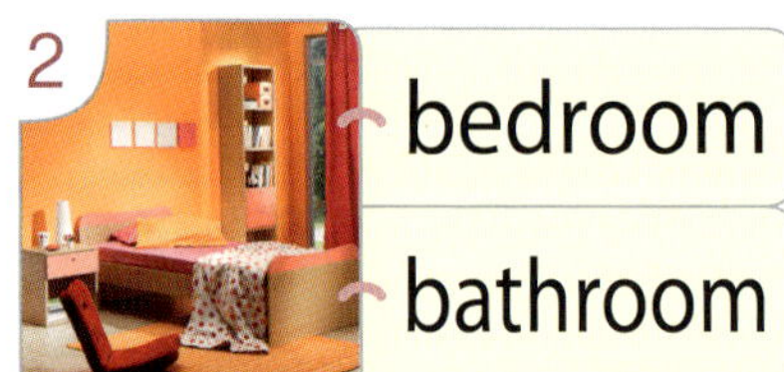
- bedroom
- bathroom

3 
- jacket
- dress

4 
- minutes
- months

5 
- music
- history

6 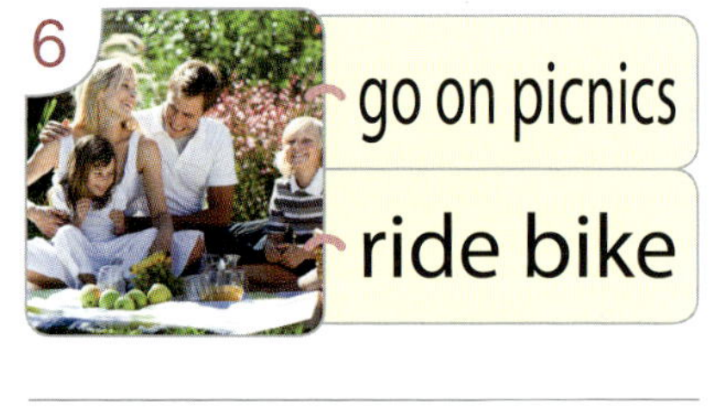
- go on picnics
- ride bike

C Look, read, and number.

❶ I ride my bike.　　❷ I'm wearing a dress.

❸ My favorite subject is music.　　❹ It takes two hours.

❺ He's in the bedroom. He's sleeping.

❻ She's in the living room. She's watching TV.

D Listen and write. Track 86

1 　subject　My　gym　is　favorite

____

2 　living room　in　the　He's

____

3 　wearing　a　sweater　I'm

____

E Read, match, and speak.

1 
What are you wearing?

I visit my grandparents. 

2
How long does it take?

I'm wearing pants. 

3
Where is Dad?

He's in the bathroom. 

4
What do you do on weekends?

It takes a long time. 

F Listen and number. Track 87

G **Circle the words you find along the way and read the sentences.
Then write the correct answer.**

Word List

cut

add

stir

fry

onion

mushroom

carrot

cucumber

tall

short

long

curly

blond

black

pretty

handsome

doll

robot

balloon

lollipop

shoes

chocolate

blocks

cake

New York

Cairo

Beijing

London

Sydney

Paris

Rome

Toronto

Statue of
Liberty

Pyramid

Great Wall
of China

Tower Bridge

Sydney
Opera House

Eiffel Tower

Coliseum

CN Tower

skirt

dress

shirt

jacket

sweater

pants

tie

socks

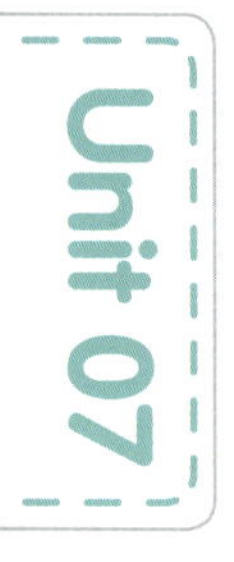

minutes

hours

days

weeks

months

years

a long time

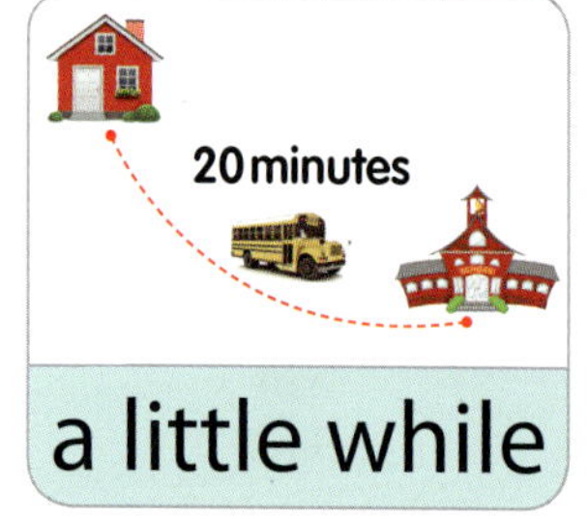

a little while

bedroom

living room

bathroom

kitchen

sleeping

watching TV

brushing his teeth

setting the table

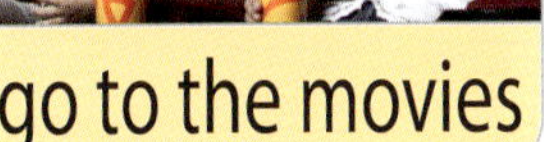

go to the movies

visit my grandparents

read books

ride my bike

play soccer

meet my friends

go on picnics

use the computer

science

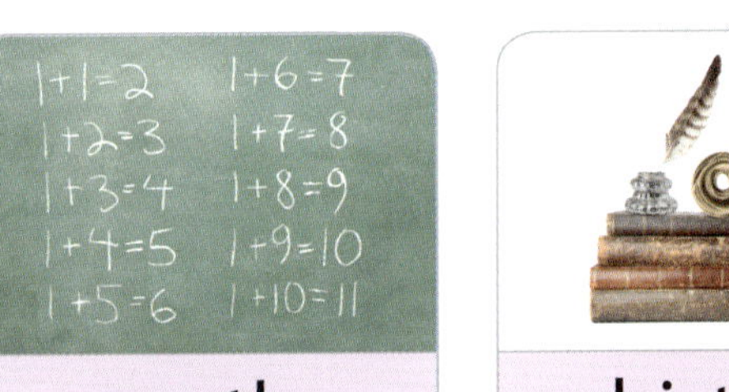

math

history

music

gym

art

interesting

fun

Written by Sarah Taylor
Illustrated by Kimberley Scott·Enrico Schacherl

First published September 2012
11th printing June 2025

Publisher: Kyudo Chung
Editors: Mija Cho, Jinhee Jeong, Mikyoung Kim, Jungwon Min
Designer: Soonam Park

Published and distributed by
Happy House, an imprint of DARAKWON, Inc.
Darakwon Bldg., 211 Munbal-ro, Paju-si, Gyeonggi-do, 10881, Republic of Korea
Tel: 82-2-736-2031(Ext. 250)   Fax: 82-2-732-2037   Homepage: www.ihappyhouse.co.kr

ISBN: 978-89-6653-082-3   68740

[Components]
• Student Book
• Workbook
(Answer Key / Audio Script / Audio Files / Word Test: free download at www.ihappyhouse.co.kr)

This book is made with nontoxic materials.

Stickers

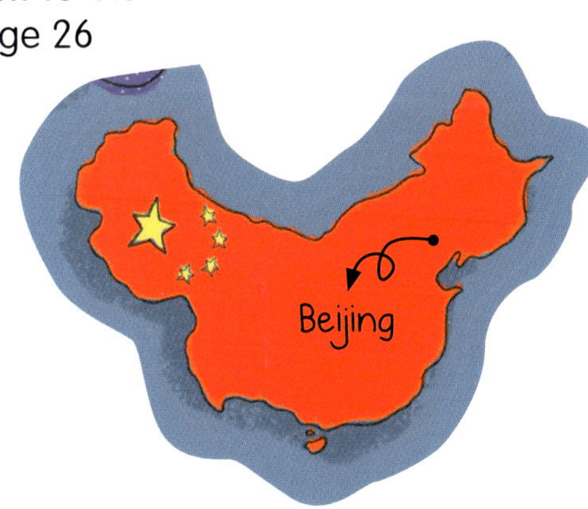

I Meet Speaking

3

Workbook

I Meet Speaking 3

Workbook

Contents

Fry the Mushrooms and Carrots

A Look, write, and speak.

1

____

2

____

3

____

4

____

5

____

6

____

7

____

8
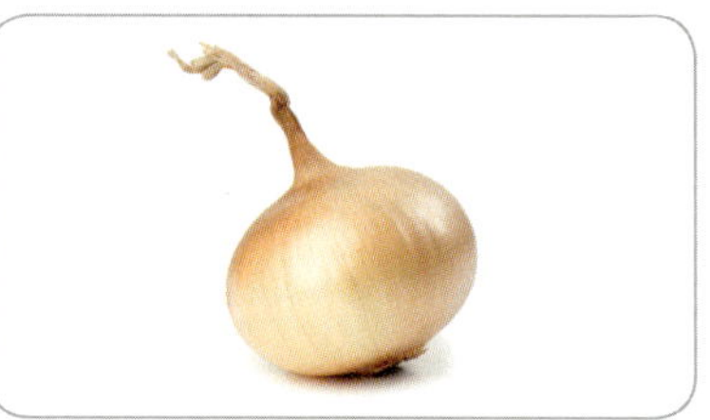
____

cut	add	fry	stir
mushroom	carrot	onion	cucumber

B Look, match, and speak.

1

Add •
• the mushrooms.

2
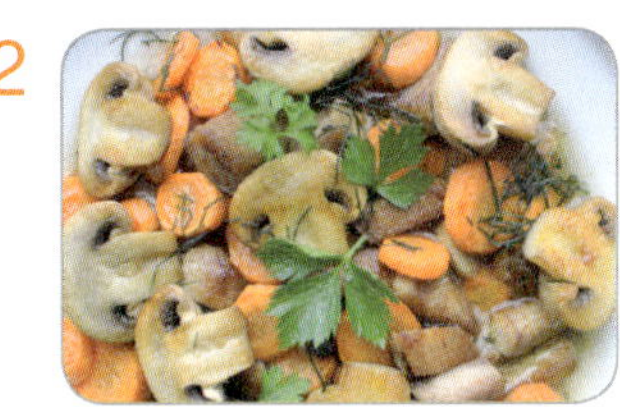
Fry •
• the cucumbers.

3

Cut •
• the mushrooms and carrots.

C Look, unscramble, and write.

1

the onions / Stir / cucumbers / and

2

Fry / and / mushrooms / the carrots

3

and / the cucumbers / Add / carrots

D Listen and number the sentences in order. Track 88

◯ Yep.

◯ Yummy!

◯ Okay.

◯ Stir the rice.

◯ Add the carrots. Where are the carrots?

◯ Let's make fried rice. Cut the cucumbers and carrots.

E Listen and write. Track 88

| Fry | cucumbers | rice | Stir | Add | Let's |

She Has Long Hair

A Look, write, and speak.

1

2

3

4

5

6

7

8

| tall | short | long | black |
| curly | pretty | handsome | blond |

B Look, match, and speak.

1 

She's pretty. •   • He has short hair.

2 

He's tall. •   • She has blond hair.

3 

She's short. •   • She has curly hair.

C Look, unscramble, and write.

1 

is / short / He

 _______________________________

2 

has / hair / black / She

 _______________________________

3 

pretty / She's / has / long / She / hair

 _______________________________

D Listen and number the sentences in order. (Track 89)

○ What does he look like?

○ I can't find my baby.

○ What does she look like?

○ I can't find my mom.

○ He's short. He has black hair. He has brown eyes.

○ She's pretty. She has blond hair.

E Listen and write. (Track 89)

hair   blond   look   handsome   tall   like

May I Have a Doll?

A Look, write, and speak.

1

2

3

4

5

6

7

8

doll	robot	balloon	lollipop
shoes	cake	chocolate	blocks

B Look, match, and speak.

1 　　May I have ●　　● some cake?

2 　　May I have ●　　● a lollipop?

3 　　May I have ●　　● a robot?

C Look, unscramble, and write.

1 

I / have / shoes? / May / some

➡ ___________________________

2 

May / have / blocks? / some / I

➡ ___________________________

3 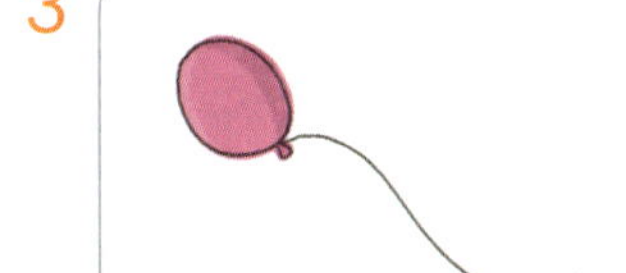

balloon? / a / I / May / have

➡ ___________________________

D Listen and number the sentences in order. Track 90

◯ May I have a hug?

◯ No, you may not.

◯ Yes, you may.

◯ May I have a doll?

◯ May I have a balloon?

◯ No, you may not.

E Listen and write. Track 90

lollipop	may	cake	balloon	chocolate	May

I Want to Visit New York

A Look, write, and speak.

1 

____

2 

____

3 

____

4 

____

5 

____

6 

____

7 

____

8 

____

| New York | Cairo | Beijing | London |
| Sydney | Paris | Rome | Toronto |

B Look, match, and speak.

1 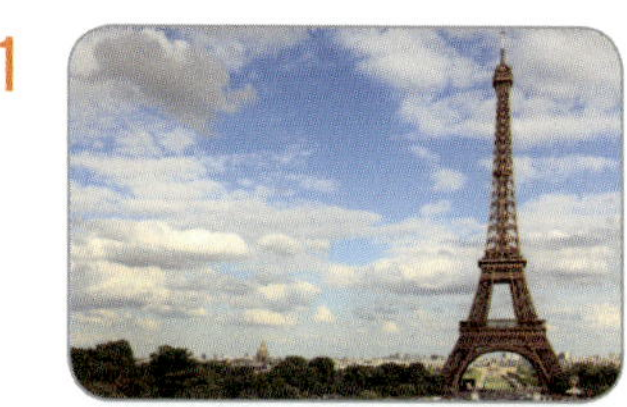 I want to visit •   • Sydney.

2  I want to visit •   • London.

3  I want to visit •   • Paris.

C Look, unscramble, and write.

1 

want / Beijing / visit / to / I

➡ _______________________________

2 

New York / to / I / want / visit

➡ _______________________________

3 

I / Paris / visit / to / want

➡ _______________________________

- It's in China.
- Where do you want to visit?
- Where is that?
- I want to visit Beijing.
- I want to visit Rome.
- Where is that?
- It's in Italy. Where do you want to visit?

E **Listen and write.** Track 91

Paris　　want　　Rome　　Where　　New York　　visit

Because I Want to See the Pyramid

A Look, write, and speak.

1

2

3

4

5

6

7

8

Eiffel Tower	Statue of Liberty	Pyramid	Great Wall of China
Tower Bridge	CN Tower	Coliseum	Sydney Opera House

B Look, circle, and speak.

1  Because I want to see the
(Eiffel Tower | Tower Bridge).

2  Because I want to see the
(Statue of Liberty | Coliseum).

3  Because I want to see the
(Pyramid | CN Tower).

C Look, unscramble, and write.

1  the Tower Bridge / Because / to / see / I / want

 __________________________________

2  the Great Wall of China / Because / see / want / I / to

____

3  Because / I / to / want / the Sydney Opera House / see

 __________________________________

D Listen and number the sentences in order.

O Because I want to see the Sydney Opera House.

O Because I want to see the Great Wall of China.
Why do you want to visit Sydney?

O Do you want to be a singer? Good luck!

O Why do you want to visit Beijing?

E Listen and write. (Track 92)

| Eiffel Tower | visit | Because | Coliseum | Why |

Review I — Units 01-05

A Find, circle, and match.

 1
 2
 3

S y d n e y u r e h a n d s o m e s h o e s i
w m u s h r o o m c u c u m b e r o c u r l y

 4
 5
 6

B Look, unscramble, and circle.

1 

2 

3 

4 

 Look, read, and check(✓).

1 

☐ She has blond hair.
☐ She has black hair.

2 

☐ Cut the onions.
☐ Fry the onions.

3 

☐ May I have a doll?
☐ May I have a lollipop?

4 

☐ Because I want to see the Coliseum.
☐ Because I want to see the Eiffel Tower.

D **Look, circle, and write.**

1 

I want to visit _______________.

Cairo | New York

2 

Cut the _______________.

carrots | mushrooms

3 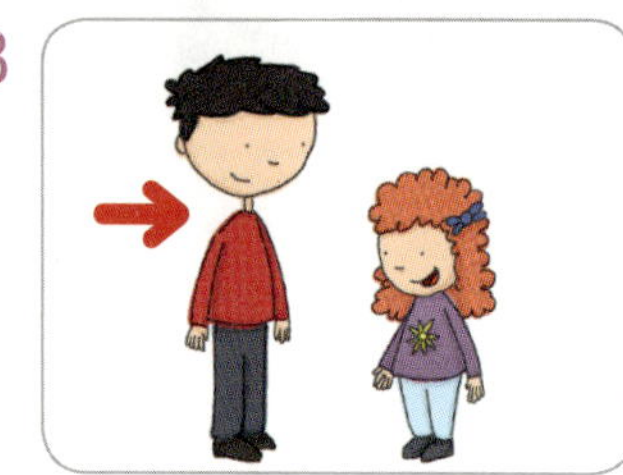

He's _________. He has _________ hair.

short | tall   black | blond

E Read and match.

1 May I have some cake?

She has long hair.

2 Why do you want to visit Rome?

Yes, you may.

3 What does she look like?

Because I want to see the Coliseum.

4 Where do you want to visit?

I want to visit Beijing.

F Look and write.

1 

Q Let's make fried rice.

A _________ the onions and _________________ .

2 

Q What does she look like?

A She's _________ . She has _________ hair.

3 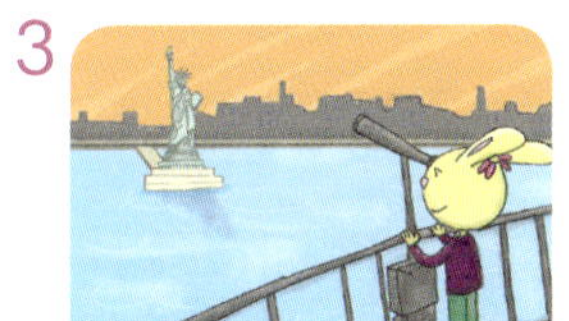

Q Why do you want to visit _________________ ?

A Because I want to see the _________________ .

| short | New York | Fry | curly | mushrooms | Statue of Liberty |

I'm Wearing a Sweater

A Look, write, and speak.

1

____

2

____

3

____

4

____

5

____

6

____

7

____

8

____

| skirt | dress | shirt | jacket |
| tie | sweater | pants | socks |

B Look, circle, and speak.

1.  I'm wearing (jacket **|** pants) and a sweater.

2.  I'm wearing a shirt and a (dress **|** tie).

3.  I'm wearing a (skirt **|** sweater) and a jacket.

C Look, unscramble, and write.

1.  a dress / I'm / wearing

   ➡ ______________________________

2.  wearing / I'm / and / a shirt / pants

    ➡ ______________________________

3.  a skirt / wearing / and / a sweater / I'm

    ➡ ______________________________

D Listen and number the sentences in order. Track 93

- I'm wearing a sweater. Do you like it?
- What are you wearing?
- I'm wearing socks.
- I'm wearing a tie.
- What are you wearing?

E Listen and write. Track 93

| shirt | dress | skirt | pants | wearing | What |

It Takes Ten Minutes

A Look, write, and speak.

1 

2 

3 

4 

5 

6 

7 

8 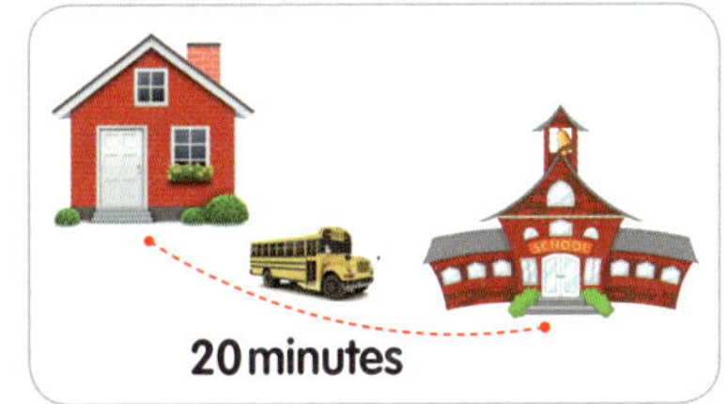

minutes	hours	days	weeks
months	years	a long time	a little while

B Look, match, and speak.

1    It takes •   • two months.

2   It takes •   • five minutes.

3   It takes •   • one year.

C Look, unscramble, and write.

1   takes / weeks / two / It

____

2    It / five / takes / days

____

3    hours / twenty four / takes / It

____

How long does it take?

It takes a long, long time.

It takes twenty minutes.
How long does it take?

It takes two weeks. How long does it take?

E **Listen and write.** (Track 94)

minutes	hour	take	long	a long time	How

Where Is Mom?

A Look, write, and speak.

1

____

2

____

3

____

4

____

5

____

6

____

7

____

8

____

| bedroom | bathroom | living room | kitchen |
| sleeping | watching TV | brushing his teeth | setting the table |

B Look, circle, and speak.

1 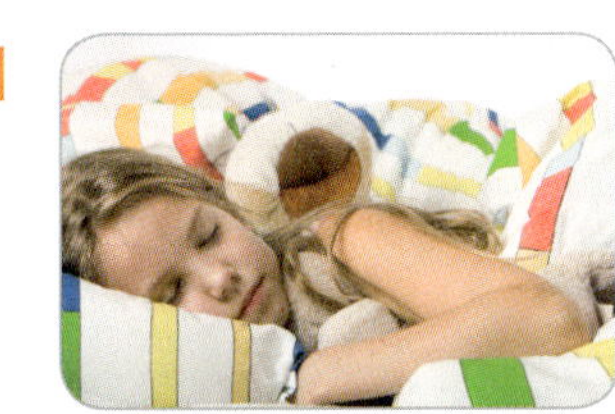

She's in the (bedroom **|** bathroom).
She's sleeping.

2 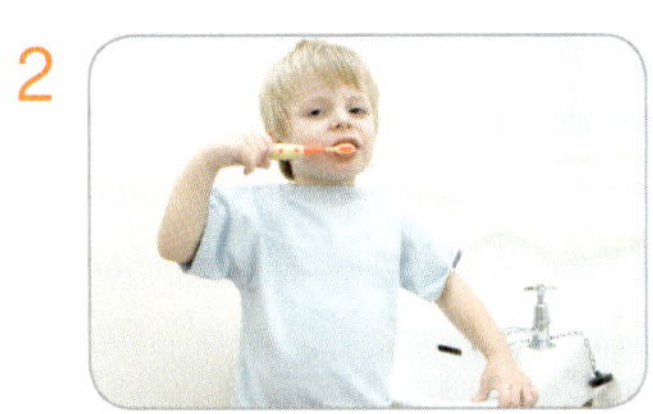

He's in the (bathroom **|** living room).
He's brushing his teeth.

3 

She's in the kitchen.
She's (setting the table **|** watching TV).

C Look, unscramble, and write.

1 

in / He's / living room / the

➡ __________________________________

2  

She's / kitchen / the / in

➡ __________________________________

3  

bedroom / in / She's / sleeping / the / She's

➡ __________________________________

D Listen and number the sentences in order. Track 95

He's in the living room. He's watching TV.

Where is Grandma?

I'm bored. Where is Dad?

I'm setting the table. Can you help me?

What are you doing?

She's in the bathroom. She's brushing her teeth.

E Listen and write. Track 95

kitchen   bathroom   bedroom   Where   brushing

What Do You Do on Weekends?

A Look, write, and speak.

1 

2 

3 

4 

5 

6 

7 

8 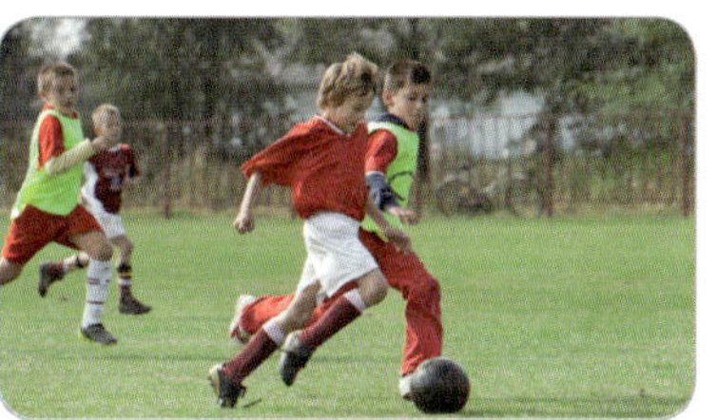

visit my grandparents	go to the movies	read books	go on picnics
use the computer	meet my friends	ride my bike	play soccer

B Look, match, and speak.

1 

I go to the movies.

2 

I use the computer.

3 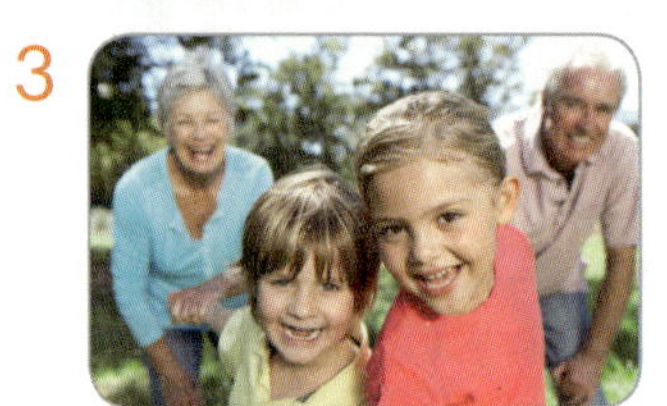

I visit my grandparents.

C Look, unscramble, and write.

What do you do on weekends?

1 

ride / I / bike / my

 _______________________________

2 

soccer / play / I

____

3 

on / I / picnics / go

 _______________________________

I visit my grandparents.
What do you do on weekends?

I meet my friends.
What do you do on weekends?

What do you do on weekends?

I use the computer.

E **Listen and write.** Track 96

| weekends | go to the movies | on | What | read books |

My Favorite Subject Is Art

A Look, write, and speak.

1

2

3

4
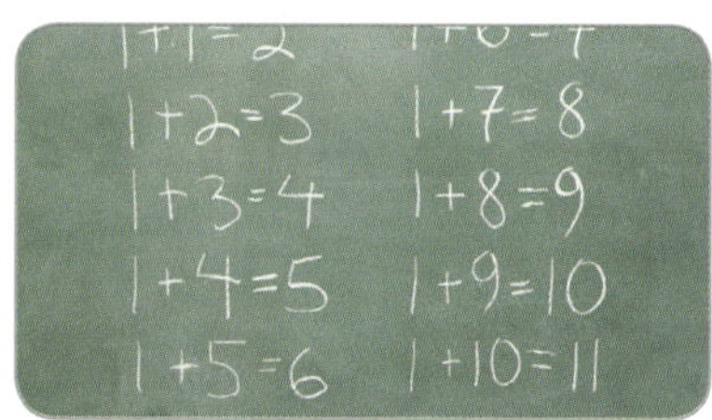

5

6

7

8

art	science	history	music
math	gym	interesting	fun

B Look, circle, and speak.

1 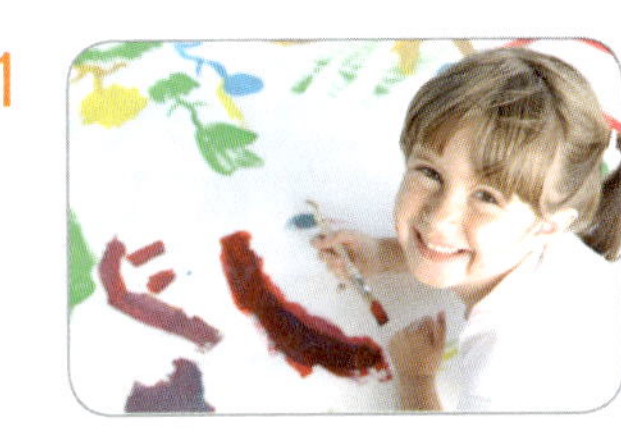 My favorite subject is (art **|** history). It's fun.

2  My favorite subject is (music **|** gym). It's fun.

3  My favorite subject is (math **|** science). It's interesting.

C Look, unscramble, and write.

1  favorite / is / My / gym / subject

 ➡ __________________________

2 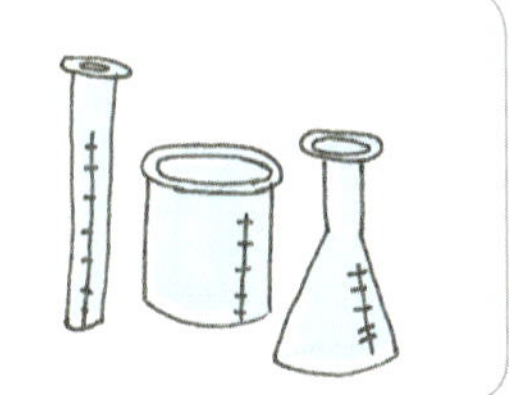 science / is / My / subject / favorite

 ➡ __________________________

3 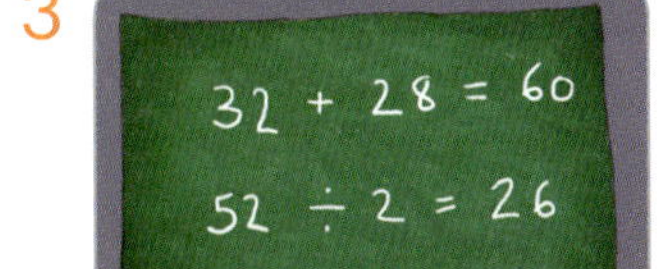 My / is / math / subject / favorite

 ➡ __________________________

D **Listen and number the sentences in order.** Track 97

- ◯ My favorite subject is gym. It's fun.
- ◯ What is your favorite subject?
- ◯ What is your favorite subject?
- ◯ My favorite subject is music. It's interesting.
- ◯ I don't like gym.

E **Listen and write.** Track 97

fun	subject	interesting	art	science	favorite

Review II Units 06-10

A Find, circle, and match.

1 
2 
3 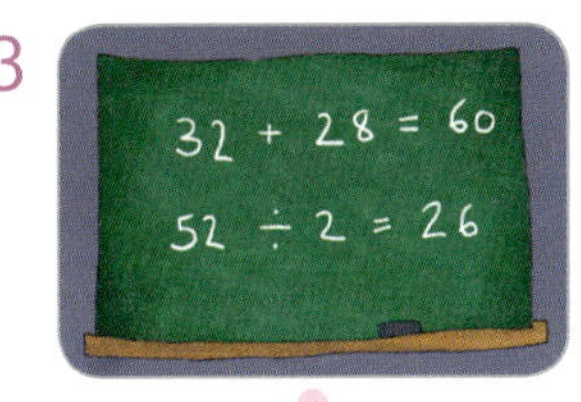

m a t h s c i e d a y s o s k i r t e s k s l
s l e e p i n g y h i s t o r y s w e s o c k s

4 
5 
6 

B Look, unscramble, and circle.

1 

boomathr

2 

rtshi

3 

icsmu

4 

thsmon

C Look, read, and check(✓).

1 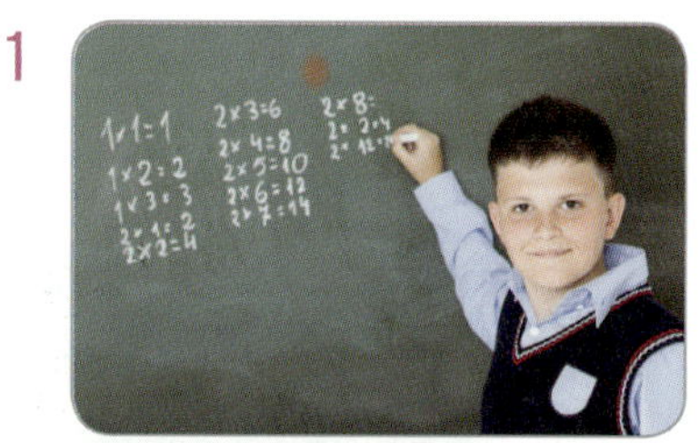

- ☐ My favorite subject is math.
- ☐ My favorite subject is gym.

2 

- ☐ I'm wearing a dress.
- ☐ I'm wearing a shirt.

3 

- ☐ I meet my friends.
- ☐ I use the computer.

4 

- ☐ She's in the bedroom.
- ☐ She's in the kitchen.

D Look, circle, and write.

1 

I ______________________.

visit my gradparents | go to the movies

2 

It takes five ______________.

weeks | minutes

3 

She's in the ______________.

bathroom | living room

She's ______________ TV.

watching | setting

E Read and match.

1. How long does it take?

2. What do you do on weekends?

3. Where is your sister?

4. What are you wearing?

I go to the movies.

It takes twenty four hours.

I'm wearing a shirt and a tie.

She's in the bathroom.

F Look and write.

1. 

   Q Where is your brother?

   A He's in the _______________.
   He's _______________.

2. 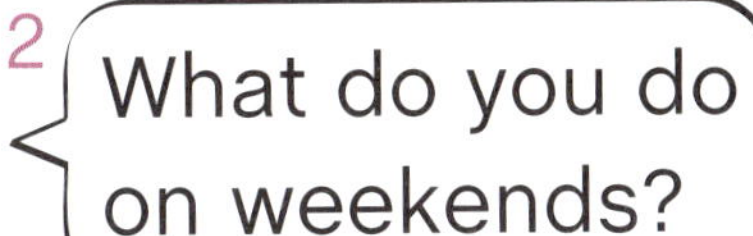

   Q How long does it _______________?

   A It takes one _______________.

3. **Q** What do you do on _______________?

   A I _______________.

| month | go on picnics | sleeping | weekends | bedroom | take |

I Meet
Speaking 3 Workbook